The Golf Bag Book

The Golf Bag Book

SCOTT MARTIN

Burford Books

Printed in the United States of America.

10   9   8   7   6   5   4   3   2   1

Library of Congress Cataloging-in-Publication Data
Martin, Scott, 1965–
    The golf bag book / Scott Martin.
            p.   cm.
    ISBN 978-1-58080-159-1
    1. Golf.   I. Title.

GV965.M29 2009
796.352—dc22   2009040269

Dedication

To G. Bruce Park (1959–2007)

CONTENTS

PART II—GOLF & OTHER GOLFERS

PART III—GOLF IS FUN

Introduction

The golf course is an odd place. A beautiful place, quite often, but an odd and even weird place. Julius Caesar, transported by time machine to the 21st Century, would feel comfortable on a road (a straight one) and he would recognize a building (with columns) and even a car would not make him feel too distant from Roman life. A salad comprising romaine lettuce, croutons, mashed anchovy fillet, and Parmesan cheese would likely be to his liking. But what would he think about golf? Surely, he would find it totally ridiculous. He would see grown men and grown women don slightly bizarre clothes, then march or plod around a park-like setting using iron weapons to hit a small ball that rarely wants to go in the intended direction. He would see torment and sorrow over this game and then find that the sorrowful and tormented can't wait to play again the next day. He would see a game where a two-inch putt counts the same as a 300 yard drive. He would also see experienced and seasoned golfers looking befuddled over matters of golf legality and golf etiquette. He would see a lot of people having a lot of fun on the golf course but he would also discover a lot of confusion, even among, or *especially* among, golfers who have been playing for years.

This book will help Julius Caesar understand golf but it will also help *you* during a moment of total confusion or serious terror when you are on the golf course. This vital tome will reveal:

➤ How to deal with a group of slow golfers that are holding you up.

➤ Your options if you hit the ball into a lateral hazard.

➤ How to recognize and appreciate the work of golf course architects, famous or otherwise.

➤ Basic golf games that will make the round a bit more fun.

➤ How to avoid death by alligator when playing in Southern climes.

➤ The basic etiquette (and rules) of match play.

➤ Key lines from *Caddyshack* and other artistically important movies.

➤ How to react appropriately when someone is jangling change in their pocket while you are putting to win the hole.

➤ How to deal, legally, with a golf ball that ends up in a big puddle in a big bunker.

➤ How to deal with a Scottish Caddie who speaks English but is otherwise totally unintelligible.

➤ How to behave after you have launched a playing partner's cell phone into a barranca because he or she was using it while you were hitting a chip (that you chunked).

➤ The real meaning, in the golf universe, of words like "chunked."

➤ And much, much more.

It's not a rules book. It's not a golf joke book. It's not a book about *Caddyshack*. It's not an etiquette book. It's simply a companion on the golf course, a friend if you like, who will not be judgmental (or mental) when it comes to real-life issues, problems, and situations that routinely occur on the golf course. If you're on the golf course and a "situation" occurs, simply reach into your golf bag and look at the table of contents. If the book fails to address your problem or issue, you can always simply throw it into a Barranca along with your friend's iPhone. The book will also help you appreciate some of the finer points of the game and the golf course. All, hopefully, without the "here's what we think you should do because we know more than you about everything" tone of a newspaper editorial.

Please enjoy the book and if you happen to come across a man dressed in a white toga looking thoroughly bemused, please point him to the bar in the clubhouse so that he can hear the joke about the guy (and you'll meet him later) who, when playing at a course where the first tee was right next to a busy road, postponed his tee shot and bowed reverently for several seconds as a funeral procession rolled along. I think that Julius Caesar would like that one.

PART I
GOLF

PRE-ROUND CHECKLIST

Roger Roger. You've got clearance Clarence. It's time to vector the golf ball in the right direction, Victor. Here's a pre-round checklist.

➤ Clubs
➤ Shoes
➤ Rain gear
➤ Pull Cart
➤ Tees (naked lady or otherwise)
➤ Ball marker
➤ Pitch Ball mark tool
➤ Balls
➤ Towel
➤ Sunscreen
➤ Hat
➤ Sense of humor and correct attitude.

If you need some of the latter, watch *Caddyshack* or *Airplane* (or both).

WARM UP STRETCHES AND DRILLS

If you can spend 15 minutes riding a stationary bicycle or elliptical machine before you play, get on the machine. When it comes to stretching, work from the ground up, starting with hamstrings and finishing with the neck. Stretching the glutes and hips can be especially important. If you can't warm up fully before your round, take two wedges and swing them for about five minutes.

When it's time to go to the range to warm up, start with chipping and trying to get the ball up and down, just like you will have to on the golf course. When working on the full swing, check all your fundamentals, then start with some pitch shots, working from 30 yards to 75 yards. Then work through all your clubs. Finally, head for the putting green. Start with some 30-foot putts, some long putts, and then some short ones, starting about a foot from the hole to build your confidence.

HOW TO DEAL WITH BAD SHOTS

The Setup

You've been hitting the ball sweetly, or at least in the correct direction, on the practice range, but when you get to the golf course, all sorts of strange things start to happen. Here's how to deal with sudden, on-course mega-disasters.

Before getting into the bad shots individually, the root of all evil when it comes to bad play is a poor set-up. Or, to put it in much more positive fashion, if you want to hit consistently decent or even better than decent shots, your set-up needs to be near-perfect. In fact, when you warm up, you should start by checking your set-up. You may not be able to hit the ball like Tiger Woods, but you *can* emulate his set-up. So, if a bad shot comes out of nowhere, start by double-checking the following.

Posture. Stand up straight, bend at the waist (keeping your back straight), then flex the knees slightly. With good posture, you should feel like you are about to guard someone in basketball.

Grip. Look down at your left hand (if you are right-handed). You should see two or three knuckles. Now look at the "V" created between thumb and forefinger. For most "average" golfers, the Vs on both hands should be pointing directly at your right shoulder. Fix this (and you should get a PGA or LPGA professional to help you) and you are well on your way to more consistent golf.

Stance. Feet should be shoulder width apart, slightly wider for lady golfers.

Alignment. Another common mistake. Go to a PGA Tour event and visit the practice range and you'll see every player using some type of alignment aid. Work on your alignment before the round. During a round you can, legally, place a club on the ground to help you get aligned before you hit a shot; however, you MUST remove the club by the time you actually hit the shot. Remember to get everything lined up: feet, knees, hips, and shoulders.

Ball position. Another major problem for most golfers, yet easily fixed. You can also check this using a club because, visually, you are presented with an optical illusion. Wedges through 8-iron: in the middle of the stance. Mid-irons (7, 6, 5, 4): one ball forward. Long irons, hybrids, and fairway woods: one ball forward. Driver and teed-up 3-wood: one ball forward, and this should be just in front of your forward heel (the left if you are right-handed).

Simply fixing your fundamentals will fix most bad shots. However, if you are on the course and things start to go from bad to worse, here are some quick fixes. But remember, after the round, book a lesson. I'll bet you a sleeve of pink Pinnacles that the professional will fix a flaw in your set up before working on your swing mechanics.

Topping

Make sure you are gripping the club with your top hand right at the butt of the club. Feel like you are keeping your spine angle consistent through the swing; your head can move laterally but it should not move much vertically. It can also help to feel that you are swinging down into the back of the ball. Note that some professional golfers are not too worried about a "thin" shot.

Fat Shots

Also known as a Roseanne (in some circles). Many golfers dip their front shoulder as they begin their backswing or turn. This often leads to a fat shot where the club meets the ground before the ball, thus covering the ball in turf and mud. As with topping, make an effort to keep the shoulders and spine angle level through the swing. A jerky swing can also lead to topping and hitting the ball fat. An on-course cure is to take an extra club (a 6-iron instead of a 7-iron) and slow down your swing. Or, at the very least, focus on making a smooth transition from backswing to down-swing.

The Lateral Shot

"Shank" is such a horrible word that it's not going to ap-pear in this book. If you hit a hosel rocket, it's a lot like get-ting a virus. The best remedy is rest and lots of liquids, followed by a session with your instructor. However, if you feel as though you should continue to play after you have sent your ball out at 85 degrees, play the rest of the round by addressing the ball on the toe of the club. If it helps, re-member that even the best golfers hit the ball where you just hit it. Note that, in addition to the sudden and imme-diate mental anguish that comes along with hitting it square, your playing partners are not going to show any mercy . . . especially if they are anything like the people who play with me.

Hitting It on the Toe

It's a lot better than the alternative! A highly technically-oriented golf instructor could probably spend an hour dis-cussing how and why you are hitting the ball on the toe of the club and what you can do to mitigate the problem but, if you are on the course, simply set up with the ball a little bit closer to the heel.

Pitching Problems

A pitch is just a smaller version of the big swing. So look above if you hit a poor pitch. Check your basics, and be sure you feel like you are keeping your spine angle constant and your shoulders level. I've seen many golfers hit poor pitch shots because they put the ball too far back in the stance. For best results, put the ball in the middle of the stance for all pitches.

Golfers tend to hit poor pitches for several reasons. Here are some common problems and some quick fixes.

➤ Ball is in the wrong place in the stance. It should be in the middle for safety.

➤ Trying to lift the pitch. Let the club do the work, and simply let the ball get in the way of the club.

➤ Trying to hit too good a shot. For most golfers, simply getting the ball on the green within 30 feet of the hole is a decent result. After a pitch, your next shot should be a putt, not a chip, pitch, or bunker shot.

➤ Backswing is too short or follow-through is too long. Imagine the shot on a clock. For a short pitch, go from eight o'clock to four o'clock. For a longer pitch go from nine o'clock to three o'clock.

➤ Stance is too open. Many golfers think that it's essential to have the body wide open to the target, yet this almost guarantees that you will cut across the ball and not make solid contact. You should be slightly open to the target, but this means pulling your front foot back about two inches from square.

For the golfer who wants to improve, the pitch shot is the hardest shot, yet it's the most important. If you're having trouble pitching, get a lesson.

Chipping Problems

Two common chipping problems are the chunk and the otherwise solid chip that only gets halfway to the hole. The chunk is a horrible feeling: the club contacts the ground about an inch before the ball, and the ball goes about an eighth of the intended distance. To ensure that it does not happen again, make sure the ball is slightly back in your stance, just inside your back foot; keep your feet together and make what almost feels like a putting stroke, with your wrists feeling like they are encased in concrete. In general, with chipping (and putting), *wrist equals risk*. Before your next chip, work on just brushing the blades of grass with the sole of the club, feeling almost no resistance. I once watched Jack Nicklaus play at a course opening and stood about ten feet from him for several holes. He said that he was a poor chipper. Of course, he never really had to chip that often because he was so good with his driver and irons, but Nicklaus always advocated chipping with one club, usually a sand-iron, and that's a mistake for the average golfer. The number one goal with a chip is to get the ball rolling as quickly as possible on the green. So, unless you have a very short chip, use an 8-iron or even a 6-iron. You want to accelerate through the ball so that it lands on a spot about three to five feet from the fringe; the ball should then roll to the hole. The best players think about holing chip shots, and you should too. If you are chipping uphill, take one more club or land the ball about 10 feet on the green instead of five. If you are chipping downhill, take a little less club, but make sure that you accelerate through the shot.

If you only have a short distance to the hole and you are just off the green, you can still chip. Just chip with a lob wedge or a gap wedge. It's a useful shot to have and when you practice the short chip with a wedge, try to hole as many of these shots as possible.

Sand Problems

I once heard a famous golf teacher say that the bunker shot is the easiest shot in the game. If it's so easy, then why is it that the top PGA Tour player in sand saves only gets up and down from a bunker two out of three times? If a professional golfer gets up and down from a bunker at least half the time, that's a result. If you have just swatted the sand six times in a bunker (slang: Colt 45) or have bladed the ball about 145 yards, then it's important to gather your thoughts and focus on some sand basics.

Next time in the bunker:

➤ Address the ball square to the target with your feet together.

➤ Open the clubface a touch, spread your feet out about a foot, and open your stance a touch. The ball should be in the middle of your stance.

➤ Imagine a small square, about 3" × 3" around the ball. Now, ignore the ball and obliterate that 3" × 3" box with a smooth swing.

One thing you should note when a good player plays a bunker shot: he or she keeps the club head accelerating through the sand. Until you become an advanced golfer, just getting the ball out of the bunker and onto the green is a significant result!

If you're in a fairway bunker:

➤ Place the ball back a ball's-length further back than normal for the club you are using

➤ Place your hands ahead of the clubhead at address

➤ Look at the front of the ball.

➤ Grip the club about half an inch down the shaft
➤ Feel that your feet and legs are quiet and
➤ Feel that you are making a swing primarily with your arms.

The cardinal rule of being in a bunker, fairway or green-side: get out!

Putting Problems

How many times have you enjoyed hitting the ball purely and sweetly all day, only to complain in the clubhouse afterward that you missed three five-footers for birdie and had six three-putts? Putting is the anti-golf for most golfers, and it's a totally different game. The implement is different. The technique is different. The mental approach is different. The demands are different. The set-up is different. The agony of a missed short putt is infinitely more agonizing than the agony of an off-target drive that finds the rough or skanky iron that ends up in a bunker. A missed two-foot putt and a short tap in equals two strokes. Yet mashing a sizzling drive and subsequently flushing a 3-iron to reach a monster uphill 450-yard par-four equals, you guessed it, two strokes. If you're looking for a game that offers statistical fairness, take up chess.

Conversely, putting offers a tremendous opportunity. It's the ultimate equalizer and provides the opportunity for a modest ball-striker to keep up with the muscular technician who can reach a monster 450-yard uphill par-four with a 3-wood and knock-down 7-iron. We have all admired Tiger Woods' game from the fairway and the tee, but Tiger Woods is the best in the world and perhaps ever because he's the *best putter*. Tiger takes putting lessons and so should you. If you're having problems on the green and you're in the men's grill complaining about all those missed short putts, it's probably because you are not taking putting lessons. And, to boot, you need to find a teacher who is a good putter and knows how to teach putting; these people are very few and far between. It's also important to have a putter that is fitted. Practice is also vital; good golfers spend almost as much time on the practice green as the range.

However, here are some quick ideas that will help you on the golf course should the wheels start to come off with the putter.

Poor Speed

One putt ends up six feet short and another zooms by the hole. In a perfect world, the putting stroke should be the same length back and through. And the length of the stroke determines the weight, or speed of the putt. If you are having problems with speed, take a practice stroke looking at the hole and thinking about the length of the stroke. Many golfers make the mistake of having a short backswing on long putts. A long putt requires a long backswing. Another speed issue comes from not hitting the ball in the putter's sweet spot. You should have the sweet spot marked on your putter. Your PGA or LPGA pro can help you with this important mark; note that the mark that came from the factory may not be accurate! Hitting a putt in the sweet spot requires sound technique, but it also means looking at the ball during the stroke. You *don't* want to think about keeping your head down during your full swing, but you *certainly* want to think about it when you are putting.

Missed Short Putts

Every great golfer misses a short putt periodically. No putting surface is perfect, and even a magnificently struck putt will veer off in the direction of Siberia for no apparent reason. If you are pushing short putts (the ball goes to the right if you are right-handed), you are probably looking up just as you are striking the ball. Keep your head down and your lower body still. If you are pulling short putts (the ball goes left), you are likely decelerating through the stroke and probably taking too long a backswing. However, if you try to push the putter through the ball, you may push the putt. So just feel as though you are making a pendulum stroke, and the putter will stay on track and will naturally accelerate through the ball.

If you are missing short putts, it could be that you are not lined up correctly. If you narrow your target, this can help. Instead of focusing just on the hole, focus on a specific blade of grass on the lip.

The easiest instant remedy for most putting ills is to keep the length of the putting stroke constant back and through. A longer putt requires a longer stroke. A shorter putt requires a shorter stroke. It's that easy. Really!

A Chronic Slice

If you are hitting banana balls all day and want a quick fix, the worst solution is to line up further and further left (for a right-hander). This makes the slice worse.

Instead, set up square to the target and close the club-face slightly. This will get you around the golf course.

You should also check your grip. Can you see two or three knuckles on the top hand? If you can't see any and you are holding the club in the palm and not at the base of the fingers, that's a big part of your problem.

Once you get off the course, set up a lesson. A chronic slicer has a hard time enjoying golf.

A Chronic Hook

A slice is more prevalent than a hook, but a hook is much worse from an aesthetic standpoint. Better players who go off the rails during a round are more likely to hit a hook than a slice.

If you are suddenly hitting vicious hooks, the best on-course advice is to take a few practice swings, feeling that the swing is smooth and rhythmic. A slow backswing followed by a supersonic downswing can often lead to a hook.

A good teaching professional can diagnose the problem creating a hook very quickly, so make sure you see a professional soon after your round.

CLUB SELECTION

How far do you hit with each club in your bag? Professional golfers know exactly how far they hit with each club, from lob wedge to driver. You should also know how far you hit with each club, which will significantly improve your distance control and lower your scores.

I was playing in the Pinehurst area a few years ago with a group of golf writers. The golf was generally atrocious, and this from a group that routinely chastises professionals for the occasional wayward shot. But that's fodder for another book. I was playing an uphill par-four. I hit a decent drive and was right in the middle of the fairway, next to the 150-yard marker. This particular course has massive greens and the pin sheet said that the hole was in the back of the green. From 150 yards, I usually use a 7-iron, maybe a 6 if I haven't had my Wheaties that morning. However, with the hole cut toward the back of a 50-yard-long green, I knew that the shot was significantly longer. To get to the real yardage, I completed the following thoroughly scientific calculation.

Yardage marked in the fairway	150
Hole location	20
Uphill to the green (and pretty steep)	15
Wind (across and hurting)	10
Real Yardage	195

When I played the course, it had just opened so the greens were a little firm so I took five off the total to come up with 190. And the yardage marker said it was 150. To hit a 190 yard shot, I take a 7-wood. So I hit a career 7-wood and was about 15 feet above the hole. I hit the downhill putt a little too hard, but it fortunately slammed into the back of the cup and disappeared for a pretty decent up-and-down and a three on the scorecard.

Said scorecard never knew that I took a 7-wood from 150 yards. Said scorecard does not care, and said golf writers had to hand me over some loot at the end of the round. Lovely!

FRUSTRATION

Watch a professional golf tournament and you'll see ample angst and plenty of frustration. I once saw a well-known professional golfer at what used to be called the Wachovia Championship four-putt from about 20 feet. Two holes later, he almost decapitated a volunteer with a sand wedge.

I haven't seen this in person but I have heard about professionals helicoptering drivers into backyards and hurling, in a discus-like fashion, putters into water hazards. Golf can be wonderfully satisfying, but it can also be massively frustrating. And frustration can quickly ruin a round of golf. It can also ruin the round(s) of your playing partner(s) if it gets out of hand. Here are some general guidelines for dealing with on-course frustration.

➤ Avoid foul language, especially if you are with a client, your boss, or you are a guest at a top club.
➤ It is never acceptable to throw a club. It's also dangerous. A golfer, as detailed in a distant edition of *Golf Digest,*

once wrapped his Big Bertha around a golf cart; the shaft snapped in two, but the great amount of energy involved allowed one part of the shaft to spring back and puncture his neck. I can't remember if he survived but if he managed to leave the emergency room alive, then you can be certain that he was murdered in the men's grill.

➤ Bad shots create frustration, and usually come from a lethal combination of a bad set-up and a ridiculously fast tempo. So, in lieu of spearing yourself with a broken shaft, check your fundamentals and make some slow, rhythmic swings.

➤ Be realistic. Golf is an incredibly difficult game to play well. A bogey on a hard hole is good result for an "average" weekend golfer. If you're a 15 handicap, breaking 90 playing by the rules of golf is a result and you should give yourself a pat on the back.

➤ Enjoy the surroundings. Turn off the cell phone/ PDA/pager/iPod/iPhone. Get out of the golf cart and walk. Appreciate that you are nowhere near mall traffic or subway congestion or a security queue at the airport or whatever annoys you the most in life. If your schedule is so hectic that you cannot practice much and you cannot take lessons as often as you would like, you need to be especially realistic about your expectations.

I've had my moments of abject frustration and I've hit some look-away-awful shots and these used to annoy me. I've missed a six-inch putt. Over the years, I've learned to laugh about these moments, and to enjoy being away from sitting at a computer typing and having to deal with solicitation phone calls from halfway around the world.

There's a lot to be said for giving up worrying about score. It's a bad obsession because one or two bad holes can quickly turn an 80 into an 88. Instead, enter Stableford competitions where a bad hole will not ruin your day. Or play match play.

A WINDY DAY

Golf is hard enough on a cloud-less day with a mere zephyr of a breeze. However, once the wind freshens, it's an added variable, or vec-tor, if you like. Better golfers enjoy the challenge and there's no reason why an av-erage golfer should not enjoy dealing with a stiff breeze.

➤ First, your score is likely to go up a bit. It's the same for your playing partners, so don't panic if it's windy.

➤ If you hit golf ball hard or try to swing hard, then the wind is going to make your life difficult. If you are play-ing into the wind and have a 150-yard shot that would normally require a 7-iron, take a 5-iron and hit the ball with an easy swing instead of trying to hit that 7-iron hard.

➤ Remember the old golf saying: into the breeze, swing with ease.

➤ If you are playing a hole with plenty of water hazards, give them an especially wide berth on a windy day.

- ➤ Wind will often dry a green, making it faster, harder, and even crusty.
- ➤ If you are playing into the wind, choke down on the club a half-inch to an inch. This will keep the ball lower and will also impart less spin on the shot.
- ➤ If you playing directly downwind, grip it and rip it!
- ➤ An "average player" will find that a strong headwind will have a significant effect, while a strong tailwind will not have a major impact. For example, if you are playing into a 25-mile-per-hour wind and you're on a 150-yard par-three, take a 4-iron or equivalent hybrid. If you are playing downwind, a wedge will not get you to the green; take an 8-iron and make a full swing.

If you play a course that's frequently windy, learn to hit some shots that will help you in the wind. The simple knock down is a friend and you can even hit the shot with a driver. See "Specialty Shots" on page 58 for a full description.

Using the Wind to Your Advantage

Good golfers know how to use the wind to their advantage, whether the wind is helping or hurting. Let's say that you're a right-handed golfer and the wind is coming from the left at 45 degrees. Aim a little left of the target and put the ball high into the wind and let the wind take the ball. If it's coming hard from the right and slightly downwind, aim slightly to the right and if you can hit a bit of a draw, hit a bit of a draw. Driving the ball into the wind is difficult and even the best golfers find it challenging; as stated above, swing easily to minimize spin. However, if you're playing an iron or fairway wood into the wind, the wind can help, provided you select the correct club. Controlling the ball downwind can be difficult, especially if the green has become rock hard. However, an approach shot into the wind means that the ball will land softly, even with a long iron; however, you have to choose the right club or else your ball will land softly, but 40 yards short of the green!

When I first started to play golf seriously, I feared the wind and found it confusing. My attitude to poor weather and serious wind has changed since, perhaps because every summer, I spend a week at Machrihanish Golf Club in Scotland. It's on the southwest coast and the wind howls in pretty much straight from Cape Cod. It will not only blow over a golf bag, but could probably blow a golf cart sideways. I like it and I enjoy the challenge of having to keep the ball under control in the tough conditions. It's frustrating at times, but pulling off some good shots on a windy day is extremely rewarding and it's one of the reasons I love playing in such weather. And let's not forget that golf is an outdoor sport and if you can't take a bit of wind from time to time, then you should probably take up darts. Or pool.

PLAYING IN THE RAIN

If there's a thundershower and there's lightning in the area, get off the golf course immediately. If you can't, then get out of the golf cart (if you're in one) and get away from the trees. Find a low spot away from a stream and stay there until the storm passes. Lightning can jump across water and through trees. You cannot. You might have a great round going, but it's not worth taking the risk as one lightning strike will likely ruin your putting for the rest of your life, if you even have one.

If lightning is not present and the rain is light, there's no excuse not to get out there on the golf course. You need the following:

➤ A waterproof hat, preferably one with a full brim. Try the Seattle Sombrero.
➤ Waterproof and breathable outerwear.
➤ Waterproof golf shoes.

➤ Wet grip gloves (available at most golf shops); these gloves work most effectively when they are wet and your grips are wet. Trust me on this; I have played in Scotland a lot.

➤ A cover for the top of your golf bag can also help.

But the most important part of playing in the rain is having a sunny attitude. I would not want to play in the rain and gales every day but every now and then, it's fun, especially if you are with a golfing buddy with a sense of humor who also likes the conditions. It helps significantly, however, if there's a hot shower and the warm fug of a comfortable pub or clubhouse waiting at the end of the round. It's here that you can laugh at the wimpy golfers who decided to stay inside because it was drizzling slightly.

Going back to lightning for a minute, Lee Trevino, one of the greatest golfers, once famously said:

"If you're caught on a golf course during a storm and are afraid of lightning, hold up a 1-iron. Not even God can hit a 1-iron."

Ironically, Lee Trevino was hit by lightning in 1975 at the Western Open on the 13th hole. Obviously, he survived, but sustained a back injury.

RULES

General Comments About the Rules of Golf

Perhaps you have visited a club or course and felt the inevitable need to micturate; your biological requirement takes you to the rest room and there, up on the wall, is a small poster with the original thirteen rules of golf. In case you need a reminder, here they are.

1. *You must tee your ball within a club's length of the hole.*
2. *Your tee must be on the ground.*
3. *You are not to change the ball which you strike off the tee.*
4. *You are not to remove stones, bones or any break club for the sake of playing your ball, except upon the fair green, and that only within a club's length of the ball.*
5. *If your ball comes among watter, or any wattery filth, you are at liberty to take out your ball and bringing it behind the hazard and teeing it, you may play it with any club and allow your adversary a stroke for so getting out your ball.*

6. *If your balls be found anywhere touching one another you are to lift the first ball till you play the last.*

7. *At holling you are to play your ball honestly at the hole, and not to play upon your adversary's ball, not lying in your way to the hole.*

8. *If you should lose your ball, by its being taken up, or any other way, you are to go back to the spot where you struck last and drop another ball and allow your adversary a stroke for the misfortune.*

9. *No man at holling his ball is to be allowed to mark his way to the hole with his club or anything else.*

10. *If a ball be stopp'd by any person, horse, dog, or any thing else, the ball so stopp'd must be played where it lyes.*

11. *If you draw your club in order to strike and proceed so far in the stroke as to be bringing down your club, if then your club should break in any way, it is to be accounted a stroke.*

12. *He whose ball lyes farthest from the hole is obliged to play first.*

13. *Neither trench, ditch, or dyke made for the preservation of the links, nor the Scholars' Holes or the soldiers' lines shall be accounted a hazard but the ball is to be taken out, teed and play'd with any iron club.*

The above originates, according to historical data (that may or may not be accurate), from around the time that the United States of America declared independence. Today's rules are, sadly, infinitely more complex and complicated. Proof comes in the form of the two books that discuss the rules. Ironically, the first, *The Rules of Golf*, is a relatively slender document, more of a booklet than a tome. The 2008–2009 version is just 180 pages including index, preamble, definitions, and appendix. There are currently 34 rules.

Clearly, lawyers wrote these rules. The language is crisp, brusque even, and the authors clearly looked at every word very closely. The goal of all legal writing should be total clarity and in this, the authors totally failed. The proof is the other book, *Decisions on the Rules of Golf*, which weighs in at 1.4 pounds and boasts a mere 600 pages. *War and Peace* by Leo Tolstoy compares at 2.5 pounds in the paperback version and is around 1400 pages. Even today, confusion reigns and further proof is the fact that most PGA and LPGA Tour players cannot get the rules totally correct and further, *further* proof is that very few USGA rules officials get 100 per cent on the official USGA Rules test.

Understanding golf rules would be significantly easier if the rules had an over-arching principle or perhaps some over-arching principles. There are none, and this only adds to the general confusion.

Perhaps the best way to provide some degree of clarity is to use specific situations, and thus this book covers some basic and common golf course events that occur from time to time.

Water and Hazards

I hit the ball into a water hazard. It's marked with yellow stakes.

If you hit the ball from the tee, you have the option to hit the ball from the tee again. The penalty is stroke and distance. The golf course may have provided a drop area. You can hit the ball from there, again with the penalty of a stroke. The language is confusing, but you can also drop behind the water hazard on an "imaginary" line extending from the hole through the point where the ball last crossed the edge of the hazard. You can go back as far as you like, but you must stay on that line.

I hit the ball into a water hazard. It's marked with red stakes.

Things get a little tricky here. All of the above from a water hazard applies. If the stakes are red, then you are in a lateral water hazard. The primary difference between a water hazard and a lateral hazard, from a rules standpoint, is that it's usually impractical or impossible to drop a ball behind a lateral water hazard. Thus if your ball enters a lateral hazard, you can drop the ball within two club lengths of the official edge (often marked by a red line) of the hazard. The penalty is one shot.

I'm in a hazard but think I have a shot. Can I play the ball?
Absolutely. However, you must not ground your club (that
is, touch the ground with your club). And there is no
penalty. It's rare for a golfer to play the ball out of a water
hazard. But many areas marked with red stakes are dry as a
bone and you can play the ball from these areas.

**I hit my ball into a stream and the current carries the
ball into an area that's out of bounds.**
Sorry, chief, it's out of bounds.

**My shot lands perilously close to out of bounds. When
I get there, the ball is right between two white stakes,
right on an imaginary line between those two stakes. Is
the ball out of bounds?**
Bad luck. You're OB (OOB in Scotland). You have to be
completely inside the imaginary line to be in bounds. However, if any part of the ball is lying in bounds, then you're
OK.

Lost Ball

**You hit the ball and you lost sight of it. When you ap-
proach the area where you think your ball landed, you
discover a hazard and can't find your ball. It seems like
the only logical conclusion is that it must have entered
the hazard.**

Here's a tricky one. You have to be honest and use some common sense. If it's clear that the ball could only have gone into the hazard, then play the next shot as if the ball entered the hazard. If there's any doubt, then you should play the ball as a lost ball.

I hit a drive and I could not find my ball.

First, especially when the course is busy, you should hit a provisional when you think that your ball is heading into deep trouble: after your first shot, drop a ball, then hit another. If you don't find the first one, you can play the second one without having to go back to the original spot, thus infuriating everyone behind you and bringing the course to a total standstill. Technically, you have five minutes to find your ball from the time you start looking for it. If you can't find it, the penalty is stroke and distance. So, let's say your second shot goes into the trees and you can't find it. You lose a stroke then you have to go back to the spot where you hit your last shot. This then becomes your fourth shot. Ouch!

I did not see my ball land. But I find a ball that I think is mine.

Every golfer should mark his or her ball. I use a Titleist and I underline the first syllable and seventh letter. At the beginning of each round, you should let your playing partners know how you mark your ball. You have to be absolutely certain that you have found your ball. If you are not totally sure, then you have, according to the rules, lost your ball and the penalty is draconian: stroke and distance.

I'm playing in the fall and I hit a decent shot that lands close to a pile of leaves that have not been swept up. I subsequently cannot find my ball.

Technically, it's a lost ball. However, many golfers sensibly declare the "leaf rule" in effect in the fall and this means that you can drop a ball where you think the ball would have ended up if there were no leaves. You can't assume that the group is using the leaf rule: you need to agree before the first shot is struck on the first tee.

Ball Movement

You're about to hit a shot and the ball moves.

What happens next depends on whether or not you have grounded your club. If your club touched the ground (not the grass) and the ball has moved, then you have to give yourself a penalty stroke, and then put the ball back in its original position. If the ball moves before you have grounded your club, there's no penalty.

I'm playing with someone and they keep moving the ball around each time they are in the fairway; they are trying to get a better lie. When I ask them about this,

they tell me that it's "winter rules" even though we're playing on July 9.

Look in the *Rules of Golf* and you'll see nothing about "Winter Rules." Some courses may dictate, at certain times of the year, that it's OK to pick the ball up, clean it, and replace it within a club length of the original position of the ball (often known as "lift, clean and place"). Clubs usually allow this only when it's wet. However, quite possibly the most important rule in golf is: *play the ball as it lies.* So you can tell your fellow golfer, with my express permission, that, by moving the ball, he has incurred too many penalty strokes to count.

Bizarre Situations

I get up to my ball and it's not in a puddle but the ground is soggy. Do I get a free drop?

If you can see water coming up from the ground either before or after you address the ball, then it's casual water and you get a free drop. You can clean your ball before taking a drop. Basically, you can take the ball to a dry place in the general vicinity of the casual water but no closer to the hole.

What happens if there is a big puddle in a bunker and my ball is in the puddle?

You get a free drop but you have to drop the ball in the bunker, no nearer the hole. If that's not possible, you still have to drop the ball in the bunker. If the entire bunker is a swimming pool, then you can play the ball as it lies (which you can always try), or you have to drop the ball outside the bunker basically along the line where it crossed into the bunker. Unfortunately, this drop will cost you a stroke as the bunker, filled to the brim with water, is now a water hazard.

I get into a bunker and the ball is sitting in a footprint that the clod who was in the bunker before me failed to rake. Can I move the ball?

I'm afraid not. That's life and if you want to wrap your driver around said clod later, that's not surprising! However, you should not follow in the footsteps of the clod and not rake the bunker. If you ever go to a PGA Tour event, watch a professional caddie rake a bunker. Caddies on the tour get fined if they don't rake the bunker perfectly; they also rake the bunker quickly.

My playing partner is closer to the hole and hits first and holes the shot! Can I do anything seeing as it was my turn to play?

You can. You can play your shot then make him or her hit the shot again! However, you may be murdered after the round. Or *during* the round.

After the fourth hole, my playing partner discovers that he has left his young daughter's short putter in his golf bag and is thus one club over the 15-club limit. What is the penalty?

If you are playing match play, then each hole that your opponent has won becomes a loss. If it's a stroke play event, the penalty is two strokes per hole with a four-stroke maximum. However, you must really dislike your opponent to enforce this rule, even if your opponent insists that he take the penalty. Playing in an official USGA event is one thing but, in general, playing a friendly round of golf is another. I always strive to play by the strict rules of golf, but I like to give my opponent a break when it comes to some of the rules that seem a bit draconian. Unless, of course, I can't stand my opponent's guts and/or he/she is a fan of a college or professional team that I absolutely abhor. Then it's strict rules.

My club has officially ignored certain rules. Can they do this?

Yes. A club can come up with "local rules" as determined by a "committee" and this means that you have to go with the local rules. You'll find these, typically, on the back of the scorecard. Sometimes, these rules can seem a hair bizarre and may need some explanation. One of the professionals will be happy to oblige.

I'd like to learn more about the rules. What's the best way to understand them fully?

I'm not convinced that it's necessary to read *Decisions on the Rules of Golf*, unless you have a month where you have absolutely nothing else on the agenda. *The Rules of Golf*, the official booklet, is more readable, but not by much. The USGA has several videos available through its website (usga.org), but I would recommend a book titled *The Rules of Golf in Plain English*. I would also recommend Peter Dobereiner's *Golf Rules Explained*. And if you get really crazy, your state golf associations often run rules seminars.

WHEN YOU'RE IN A BAD SPOT

Johnny Miller is one of the all-time greats of golf and has taken up commentary with NBC where he is, to put it mildly, somewhat controversial. However, he once wrote that "if you're in trouble, get out of trouble." That's great advice, even for great golfers. If you go to a professional tournament, you will often see the top golfers being extremely successful. Yes, some will go for the low percentage shot but, most of the time, a professional will pitch out and get a bogey instead of attempting a risky shot that might lead to a triple bogey. So, here are some easy ways to get back in play when a poor shot puts you in a bad spot. A conservative approach will ultimately lead to lower scores, and you'll be amazed at how often you end up with a par after pitching out and getting the ball back in play.

Behind a Tree

Perhaps you've heard the old cliché that trees are 90 percent air. That may be true, but no golfer has been able to hit a golf ball through a tree. The best strategy is to hit a pitch back into the fairway. If you have to get the ball under some low branches, take an 8-iron, put the ball back in your stance and make sure that you hit the ball first before the ground. You only need a short swing, and make sure that you accelerate through the ball. If your ball is in pine needles, you need to play the ball further back in your stance. If you have a bit more of a window, then you should use a pitching wedge or gap wedge instead of an 8-iron.

In Deep Rough

If the ball is in the rough, you have to make a decision about how far you can advance the ball. In light rough with a good lie, you can often hit a normal shot. A lot depends on the type of grass. Three inches of bermudagrass rough is a lot tougher than three inches of rye grass rough. If you're in Scotland and you're in some of that deep stuff that looks like hay and is referred to as the "jungle," then you absolutely need to hack it out. Take your sand wedge, open the face, and make a strong swing. Use the same technique if you're in deep bermudagrass rough. It's a huge mistake to think that you can take out a hybrid or high-lofted fairway wood and hit the green. Hybrids are excellent clubs and help many golfers, but you should ignore the part of the advertising copy that says that the club will make it easy to get the ball out of the rough.

On Hardpan

If you miss the fairway, you may find yourself on bare ground, also known as hardpan. Good players actually like this type of lie because it's easier to impart major spin on the ball. However, the average player should not panic. It's ultra-important to hit the ball first, and a thin shot from hardpan is not a bad result. Put the ball back a little in your stance and make a smooth swing; it may help to feel that you are swinging down into the back of the ball.

Under the Lip in a Fairway Bunker

When the average golfer hits a successful bunker shot, the ball will come out lower than usual. So if you are close to the lip, getting the ball up in the air and onto the green is a risky proposition. You are much better off simply taking a lofted club and getting out of the bunker and onto the fairway.

The 40-Yard Bunker Shot

A short bunker shot is much easier than a 40-yard bunker shot. However, the shot is not impossible and is even enjoyable when you pull it off; successful execution requires the correct technique.

➤ The ball should be in the middle of your stance and your feet, hips, and shoulders should be slightly open.

➤ Instead of using a lob wedge, take a 9-iron or even an 8-iron if you don't need to get the ball high in the air.

➤ Just open the clubface a hair and then make a normal bunker swing, making sure that the clubhead gets into the sand before the ball.

In a Divot

It may seem totally unfair to find yourself in a divot after hitting a great drive. But that's life and you have to play the ball as it lies. Simply make a normal swing and aim to make the divot bigger. It's not that hard a shot. Increasingly, many golf courses are filling divots with sand and seed mix, and have a local rule that you can take a free drop out of a sand-filled divot.

Get to 100 Yards

One common mistake that many average and weekend golfers make is to hit a recovery shot to around 40 to 60 yards. For the average or weekend golfer, this distance is tricky and requires a difficult pitch. You are better off to aim to get the ball to around 100 yards, or whatever is your typical wedge distance. It's quite often better to hit a full shot with a wedge than a half shot.

SPECIALTY SHOTS

It's always fun to have some tricks up your sleeve when you are playing golf. Hitting some "specialty shots" can be fun, especially when you pull off the shot. Here are a few of these shots: just make sure that you practice these before taking them to the course.

Hitting Left-Handed (if you're right-handed) from behind a tree or other obstacle.

Take your normal right-handed grip, and simply turn the club upside down. Use a short-iron and take a simple, short swing only backwards. Your aim is to make contact and if you're successful, then the ball will squirt out.

Bouncing a Ball Off a Wall

If you're playing a quirky golf course with a building on or right next to the course, then you might need this shot. Use a pitching wedge and make a short punchy swing; then simply bounce the ball into the building or wall. You may also need this shot if you're playing the famous Road Hole (17th) at St. Andrews (Old Course).

A Tricky Spot Just Off the Green

If you play a course like Pinehurst #2 or if you go to a course in Scotland, you are going to find some very tricky green complexes. This means you could hit a decent shot just off the green, only to face a difficult recovery shot. Maybe there's a small mound between you and the ball. Perhaps there's a swale. Maybe you're at the bottom of a steep bank. If you are not sure how to proceed, use your putter and, most importantly, use your imagination. If your lie is good and you feel comfortable with a lob wedge, a short pitch with some spin can be tremendously effective. If you have some room between you and the hole, then a long chip can be a good option. If you are at the bottom of a steep bank, take a 7-iron, put the ball well back in your stance, and hit a firm punch right into the base of bank; the ball will pop up, climb the bank, and tumble onto the green. It's a fun shot (when executed). Be relatively conservative, and just try to get the ball within 10 feet of the hole relatively safely.

The Knockdown Shot

The simple knockdown is a friend, especially when it's windy, and you can even hit the shot with a driver.

➤ Place the ball a little further back in your stance than normal. Put your weight on your front foot, and keep it there.

➤ At address, put your hands forward a little.

➤ Now make a controlled swing, feeling like you are simply swinging with your arms and torso, while keeping your lower body quiet.

It's actually more of a punch than a knockdown, but it's an effective shot on a windy day. And the shot, when executed properly, reduces side spin, which is especially important if the wind is howling across the hole, left to right or right to left. If you are right-handed and you hit a slice and the wind is howling left to right, then the wind is going to take the ball completely across the entire the golf course into the next county.

Getting Out of a Pot Bunker

The best advice when it comes to getting out of a pot bunker is to avoid getting in them. But even Tiger Woods gets in them. Sometimes, you may have a clean lie in the middle of the bunker and it will be relatively easy to get out; just hit a normal bunker shot. However, remember to be conservative and make getting out of the bunker your first priority, even if it means hitting out backwards. If you are close to the front lip of the bunker, hit a regular bunker shot but leave the club in the sand on the fol-low-through, which means, of course, that it's not really a regular bunker shot.

DEALING WITH AN ESPECIALLY DIFFICULT HOLE WITHOUT PILING UP A BIG NUMBER

If you are facing an especially difficult hole, perhaps with difficult weather conditions, be realistic. The hardest hole I think I've ever played is the 9th at the wonderful Bald Head Island near Southport on the North Carolina coast. It's about 444 yards and it's a par-four. On a windy day, I'd like to see a really good professional par the hole. The drive plays to a thin island fairway that's crowned. The hole usually plays into a howling gale, so getting to and staying on the fairway requires a career shot. The approach is no picnic; there's a wetland area about 60 yards in front of the green and while the green is relatively flat, there are plenty of greenside bunkers. I'm usually delighted with a five here and I'm perfectly happy to play the hole as a par-five. I take a fairway wood off the tee, hit a punch of some sort to about 100 yards, then hit another punch for the approach, then get down in two.

So, if you are playing a really treacherous hole, give it a wide berth. If it's a par-four or a par-five and you can get to 100 yards in three shots for a par-four or four shots for a par-five, then you've been successful, and should give yourself a pat on the back. The worst that will (or should) happen from a 100 yards is a bogey, and there are times when you will get up and down from 100 yards to card an excellent par.

What about horrible par-threes? Thankfully, holes like the 17th at the TPC Sawgrass are extremely rare. If every par-three required a heroic shot like the one required there, nobody would play golf. Most difficult par-threes have some wiggle room and, once again, there's nothing wrong with a four on a difficult par-three, especially if you're an average or "weekend" golfer. Take plenty of club, aim for the middle of the green, or well away from the trouble, and let your short game take over.

When it comes to expectations, here are some general guidelines that will help you enjoy the difficult and not-so-difficult.

➤ A good player (handicap plus to 5) should aim to birdie every hole.

➤ A decent player (handicap 5 to 12) should aim to par or birdie the easier holes but be happy with a bogey on a very hard hole.

➤ The average player (12 to 20) should be happy with the occasional par and a bogey on most holes.

➤ The "improving" golfer (20 and above) should throw a party after a par and be delighted with bogey.

Be realistic about your expectations in golf (and pretty much everything else) and you'll enjoy the game a lot more.

READING A GREEN

On television, during a golf tournament, the person operating the camera will sometimes get a great shot of a putt from directly behind the line of the putt. And then the producer will run the putt in slow motion; you will see the ball bouncing, wobbling, waddling, and moving around; even a tour-quality green has imperfections. So, quite often, when you miss a putt, it's because the green is not smooth. That's life. Get used to it.

However, if you learn how to read greens (and it's more science than art) then your chances of making some putts increase, and if you make five more putts than you normally might, that 89 quickly becomes an 84.

All greens have grain, but some greens have more grain than others. In the United States, greens are sewn with either bentgrass or bermudagrass. You'll find bentgrass where it tends to be cold in the winter, and you'll find bermudagrass greens in warm and hot climates (from

Florida to Phoenix). In certain locations, especially northern California, you'll find Poa Annua. For green reading purposes, you only have to worry about grain in any significant way when you are playing on bermudagrass greens. Modern agronomy has produced several new strains of bermudagrass that are smoother and less grainy. However, if you are playing on bermudagrass greens, here are some general tips.

➤ Look for a significant geographical feature like a mountain or a river. Ask the starter or the pro in the golf shop about the main influence. Grain will often run away from a mountain toward a river.

➤ Toward the end of the day, grain will grow toward the sun.

➤ Look for sheen and areas that look greener. If the green is shiny as you look at it, the grain is going away from you. If it's really green and dense, then you are putting into the grain.

➤ Putts down grain will be fast.

➤ Putts into the grain will be slow.

➤ Grain can affect short putts and, as the grain has more influence on the ball as it slows, there's nothing wrong with hitting short putts firmly to the back of the cup . . . unless you miss the putt and it starts rolling down grain.

Reading grain is extremely difficult. I can remember recently playing on a course with some very grainy bermudagrass greens. I was playing with two other golfers, and we all hit good shots to a par-three over water. I was the furthest away, about 20 feet from the hole, which was cut on a slight down slope at the front of the green. I thought that it might be grainy due to some definite sheen, and I hit the putt delicately and well above the hole. I think it's still rolling: the grain took it and I might as well have been putting on an icy ski run.

If a green has a noticeable slope, sometimes it can be relatively easy to read the putt. Reading greens becomes harder when a green has tiers or looks like it's been constructed by a drunk who was told to make the green dead flat. You are going to get the best read from below the hole and below the line of the putt. However, the most important piece of advice when it comes to reading greens came during a lesson I took from Julie Cole at The Dana Rader Golf School at Ballantyne Resort in Charlotte, North Carolina. She simply said, "Listen to your feet."

So, when you can, walk up and down the length of the putt (without slowing down the pace of your round), and your feet will tell you whether it's uphill or downhill.

Playing the same course regularly is a bonus when it comes to reading greens: the putts are always going to break in the same direction. However, there is no substitute for practice. The putters who always seem to be able to read the greens with the most accuracy are the ones that practice the most. Funny how that works!

PRACTICING

If only those of us who are not professional golfers had hours and hours to practice. In reality, most of us are for- tunate to get an hour in each week. And most golfers I see use 50 minutes of that 60 trying to smash long drives with the driver. That's a mistake. Every mid-handicap golfer's goal should be to turn four shots into three, and every good golfer's goal should be to turn three shots into two. The best way to achieve these goals is around the green, and so at least 30 minutes out of every hour should be spent working on putting, chipping, pitching, and sand play.

When you work on your short game, it's a mistake to sit in one position and hit the same shot 20 times. It is best to practice real-life situations, so go to different parts of the practice green and try to get up and down. There's nothing wrong with trying to make every shot around the green; if you chip the ball in the hole when you are practicing, it could easily happen on the golf course, and chipping the ball in the hole during a round is the best way to irritate your opponents. Trust me on that one.

Long game practice should follow a plan. Start with wedges and work up to long-irons, woods, and then the driver. Work on what your teacher told you during your last lesson. In general, focus on hitting a few good shots rather than simply smashing as many balls as possible. And remember to focus on fundamentals and target awareness. Have some fun with your practice: for the last 15 minutes, pretend that you are playing your favorite course.

COURSE MANAGEMENT

How many times have you been watching a golf tournament on the television and heard this cliché?

That was good course management.

And how often have you asked, "What on earth does that mean?"

No, it has nothing to do with the agronomic skills of the golfer, but instead refers to the navigational skills, if you like, of the golfer. You can learn a lot from these navigational skills and, aside from short game work, the fastest way to lower your score is to be a better navigator.

For the most part, good course management simply means being sensible. For example, if you are not a great golfer and you have the choice off the tee of hitting the ball close to a water hazard to make the hole a little shorter, or hitting the ball to the fat part of the fairway, good course management dictates that you should hit the shot to the fat part of the fairway. If you are in the woods and there's really only one way out, even if it's backwards, then good course management is to get the ball back into play. If you're a better player and you hit your irons very well, then you might want to start trying to hit the ball close to the hole, but only when the hole is accessible: i.e. not right next to a deep pot bunker.

I can't say that I'm the world's greatest course manager but I quite often find that, if I play like I have a caddy with me, that my course management improves and I shoot lower scores. A good caddy can quickly size up your game and point you in the right direction; yes, smashing the ball a long way is fun but a good course manager knows and understands that a five on a par-four is better than a seven or an eight. A poor course manager routinely writes checks that he cannot cash—at least from a golfing standpoint. If I really want to needle an opponent on the golf course, I might (in total jest) say: "your golf mind wrote a check that your golf ability could not cash." That's a polite way of saying, "your course management is shockingly awful."

ALLIGATOR ATTACK

If you are playing golf on the South Carolina coast, the Deep South, or in Florida (or perhaps in other regions), you will likely see an alligator if you are playing at the coast or near some wetlands. Alligators rarely attack golfers, and you are statistically more likely to have a hole-in-one than find a large reptilian swamp-dweller chasing you down the fairway. However, alligators are extremely fast and can run you down.

If you suddenly find yourself under attack, don't panic: you should run away, of course, but run as if you are completing a slalom at your favorite ski resort; alligators can be quick in a straight line but once you start to turn left and then right, they cannot move sideways and will likely, hopefully, give up.

The question remains, though; what's more impressive, a hole-in-one or surviving an alligator attack? James Bond, in *Live and Let Die*, got through the latter and while we know he played golf, there's no known record of a 007 hole-in-one. So, if you score an ace, you can say that you're better than James Bond, but if you escape a bad situation involving alligators then you can say that you're *better* than James Bond.

A wild turkey once attacked me at a course in the Pinehurst area. I fended it off, rapier-like, with a gap wedge.

LIGHTNING— WHEN YOU'RE NOWHERE NEAR THE CLUB HOUSE

If your golf course has designated lightning shelters, head for one of these. If there is no shelter and you are really in the middle of nowhere, avoid trees, head for the shallowest ground around you, and lie down. Yes, you may get soaking wet, but at least you won't be dead. And ditch the golf cart quickly. Ditto the umbrella. Avoid water totally: lightning has been known to jump across water; just ask Lee Trevino.

PART II
GOLF & OTHER GOLFERS

THE BASIC RULES OF GOLF ETIQUETTE

1. Play quickly.
2. Cell phone off.
3. Stay still and remain totally silent when your playing partner is about to hit a shot.
4. Do not helicopter clubs; leave that to John Daly et. al.
5. Ready golf is always a good idea during friendly and casual golf.
6. Rake bunkers. Repair pitch marks. Fix divots.
7. Be good company at all times.
8. If you have been the guest of a member at a club, write a thank you note.

ETIQUETTE

In my golfing travels, I've come across plenty of people who get really irritated when it comes to golf etiquette and expect everyone to be perfect all the time, but I have *never* come across *anyone* who has demonstrated perfect etiquette. So, perhaps the first rule of etiquette is tolerance.

Of course, that's tough. I remember playing in a tournament at the wonderful Mid Pines in the Pinehurst area. I was not having a great day and I was not in the best mood. One of the people in my group could not keep his mouth shut and would keep talking (about absolutely nothing) while other people were putting, driving, chipping, etc. One of the beautiful aspects of the Pinehurst area is quiet solitude among the loblolly pines. This lack of ambient noise also means that it's possible to hear what someone is saying from about 50 yards away, even if they are whispering.

The 15th at Mid Pines is a 488-yard par-five that's downhill and usually a birdie hole. The first step toward that four is a drive down the middle of a fairway that's the widest in the Pinehurst area. However, I had missed the fairway, found myself behind a tree, and had to scramble, but got to a spot just in front of the green in four shots. I was getting ready to chip, but the non-stop talking golfer was talking about who might be the best high school quarterback in North Carolina. He was whispering but, in my state of mind, it sounded like a Roseanne scream. I stepped away. He kept talking. I stepped away once again. He kept talking. So I finally yelled: "WILL YOU SHUT UP FOR ONCE! I'VE BEEN LISTENING TO YOU BLAB ON FOR THE LAST 14 HOLES AND I'M SICK AND TIRED OF IT. DON'T YOU KNOW THAT YOU'RE SUPPOSED TO BE QUIET WHEN OTHER PEOPLE ARE PLAYING?"

This rare outburst kept the individual quiet for about ten seconds, enough time for me to chip the ball into the hole for a routine par. After the outburst, I had to chip the ball in; I *had* to!

The non-stop talker's etiquette, throughout the round, was, of course, horrific. Golf requires some degree of concentration, and it's almost impossible to go through all the thoughts that go through the head of the average golfer while someone is talking about the scintillating subject of high school quarterbacks. I have to admit, albeit reluctantly, that my golf etiquette was horrible. Not *equally* horrible, but horrible nonetheless. In retrospect, I would have been better off simply taking the non-stop talker aside and politely telling him that he's been talking non-stop while other people have playing their shots. I'm not sure this would have worked, but it's better than screaming. Especially in the Pinehurst area, which is all about quiet, peace, and total serenity.

Before dealing with the basics of good etiquette, here is a general guide to how to deal with people who are consistently breaking the "rules" even though the "rules" are unwritten and there are no penalties involved.

Life is a lot easier if you are playing with more than two people. In this instance, you can quietly take the person aside and say, "on the last hole, you walked right in the line of Allan's putt." In most cases, for most golfers, this will get the etiquette side of the brain working, and the golfer will be on best behavior the rest of the round. The vast majority of golfers want to be known for having exemplary manners on the golf course.

If it's just you and one other person, you have an opportunity for a little bit of revenge. Let's say that your playing partner has just walked on your line or has let his Blackberry ring while you are putting. You should express your dissatisfaction with the obvious breach of etiquette. However, you should wait until the perfect moment. I would recommend just before he or she is about to tee off. Or just before a putt. Yes, it's a bit dastardly but you have to make your point sometime. Right? And if you don't want this happening to you, then follow the proper etiquette.

Here's another way to get your opponent(s) in line. Billy Joe Patton lives in Morganton, North Carolina. He was a tremendous amateur and almost won the Masters in 1954. One day, he was playing at his home course, Mimosa Hills, with two male members and a young, talented junior named Dana Rader. Billy Joe and Dana were teamed up against the members and Billy Joe had to make a putt. Just before sinking it, he said to Dana, "Dana, if that guy will stop jangling change in his pocket, I might be able to make this putt." Billy Joe could back up that type of talk so, if you decide to follow the same route, make sure you can put as well as, or nearly as well as, Billy Joe. Start practicing!

THE NEEDLE (GAMESMAN- SHIP)

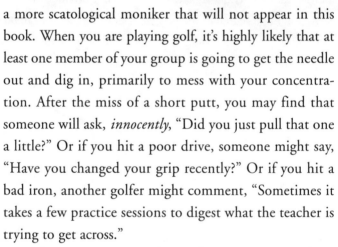

In the United Kingdom, it's called chirping. In the United States, it has a more scatological moniker that will not appear in this book. When you are playing golf, it's highly likely that at least one member of your group is going to get the needle out and dig in, primarily to mess with your concentration. After the miss of a short putt, you may find that someone will ask, *innocently*, "Did you just pull that one a little?" Or if you hit a poor drive, someone might say, "Have you changed your grip recently?" Or if you hit a bad iron, another golfer might comment, "Sometimes it takes a few practice sessions to digest what the teacher is trying to get across."

Of course, sometimes the needle is not quite so subtle. It can be annoying and even distracting. I'm all for good manners and superb etiquette on the golf course, and the best way to keep the needler quiet is to make those short putts and hit consistently good shots. However, if the needler is still needling, send it back his or her way. Here are some lines for you, and all should be delivered after a poor or mediocre shot.

If the needler has clearly spent a lot of money on golf clubs:
"Have you had those irons custom-fitted? Are you sure you went to the right guy?"

If the needler has clearly spent a lot of money on golf clothing:
"Those are the pants that Jesper Parnevik wears, right?"

If the needler hits a ball deep into the woods:
"You can still make par from there."

If the needler misses a short putt:
"I probably should have given that one to you."

If the needler duffs a chip:
"Make sure you fix your divot."

If the needler hits a really poor shot:
"You've been watching Joe Pesci play golf, haven't you?"

If the needler hits a put that lips out:
"That's tough. In and out. Just like a shot in basketball that looks like it's going in."

If the needler slices the ball into the woods:
"Gambling is illegal at Bushwood."

Anyone with even a decent imagination can come up with some more.

WHEN AND WHEN NOT TO CONCEDE A PUTT

You know how it goes: your opponent hits a shot that ends up close to the hole. It's decision time: concede, or make him or her putt? It's a controversial subject; poor putters and poor competitors ask for, or even demand, that you rake the putt back to them. Even the best miss short putts and a one-foot putt counts the same as a big drive, so you have every right to make the other person putt. Here are some basic guidelines should you find yourself in a concession quandary.

➤ Remember that the goal of the game is to get the ball *into* the hole.
➤ Only really, really awful golfers ask for a concession.
➤ If your opponent asks for a concession, he or she does not want to putt. Make them putt the ball.

It's terrible etiquette to demand a concession.

WHEN SOMEONE OFFERS YOU UNSOLICITED INSTRUC-TIONAL ADVICE

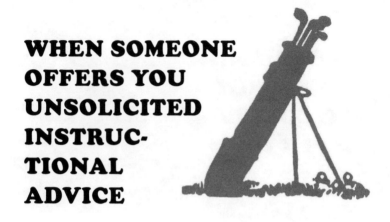

Advice in golf can come anywhere at anytime. You could be in the dentist's office. Or the supermarket. Or a public lavatory in Scotland. Or a Christmas party at The White House. Advice often comes from fellow golfers, and it's highly unlikely that the person handing out the advice is a PGA or LPGA teaching professional. How do I know this? A PGA or LPGA teaching professional would not hand out unsolicited advice.

If you are having a hard time on the course and some-one offers advice, it's highly likely that they are giving you the needle. Ignore that. They could be trying to help, but ei-ther way, ignore the advice and focus on making sure that your fundamentals are correct and that you are swinging slowly and smoothly with a consistent spine angle.

YOU'RE PLAYING WITH SOMEONE WHO PLAYS RARELY AND HAS NOT ESTABLISHED A HANDICAP BUT STILL WANTS A GAME

There are two ways to go if you are playing with someone who hardly ever plays and looks like a real duffer. The first is to give them two shots a hole, every hole. The second is to use what's sometimes called "The Sunningdale" handicap. If your opponent goes two shots down, he or she gets a stroke. If your opponent goes three or more strokes down, he or she gets two strokes. The latter is remarkably effective at keeping a game close.

YOUR SIGNIFI-CANT OTHER IS WITH YOU, AND IT'S QUICKLY BECOMING A DISASTER

There is no easy solution to this problem. And it's a definite problem. After nine holes, you may wish to say, "Look, why don't you wait here while I finish the round." However, at the end of 18 holes, you may be facing the wrong end of a bazooka. The other alternative is to go to this web site: *www.drphil.com.*

GOLF GAMBLING GAMES

Nassau

The most common golf gambling game is the Nassau. There are three competitions: one for the front nine; one for the back nine; one for the 18 holes. It's match play. You can play $5 for the front, $5 for the back, $10 for the 18. It's not always that simple though, as you can add the "press," which means that if you lose one of the bets, you can start a new bet. Some golfers play an automatic two-down press. It can get extremely complicated, and it seems that each and every golfer has his or her own personal variations. If you are getting into a Nassau, pay very close to attention to the details. I once played Nassau where it was $10 for the front, $10 for the back, and $20 for the eighteen. My partner and I played well on the front but not so well on the back, and my partner was in charge of tallying up the bets. Fortunately, I chipped in for a birdie on the 18th; if I had not, I would have forked over $400. Instead, the damage was just $30. You've been warned!

Here's how it works. Let's say you have a relatively even game going but you win the 8th hole to go one up, and it stays that way after the ninth hole. You have won the front nine and you are also one up in the main game for 18 holes. Let's say that you lose the 13th and 14th and all the other holes are even. You lose the back nine and also the 18 holes.

Trash

Some golfers add some additional items to the Nassau and you dictate an amount for each element of trash.

Birdie. No explanation needed.
Eagle. Can be up to 10 times the value of a birdie.
Sandy. Up and down for a par from a greenside bunker.
Murphy. Up and down for par.
Poley. A made putt longer than the flag stick.
Barkey. A par or better made after hitting any part of a tree.

Again, golfers have their own variations. In the United Kingdom, golfers call trash . . . "bits."

If you lose, always pay up. If you win the money, buy the first round of drinks in the bar, especially if you're in the United Kingdom.

Skins

Skins is also a popular game. It's match play also. If you win a hole, you get a skin. However, if the hole is halved, then the skin carries over to the next hole. So, technically, you could tie the first 17 holes, and then the winner of the 18th hole would get all 18 skins. Skins works well if you have three players but can also work for four or two.

Stableford

If you have a big group or if you have three people and want to play more of a stroke play game, then the Stableford system works well and keeps play moving along quite well. Instead of a score, you get points, based on handicap.

Albatross (double-eagle): 5 points
Eagle: 4 points
Birdie: 3 points
Par: 2 points
Bogey: 1 point
Double bogey or worse: 0

Obviously, the person with the most points wins the loot.

Foursomes (Alternate Shot)

If you have four players and you don't have much time and the golf course is relatively clear, then alternate shot is fun. You may have seen it at The Ryder Cup. One player tees off on the even holes, the other tees off on the odd holes; the golfers take turns hitting shots until they hole out. You can play match play, or a stableford.

Foursomes is especially popular in the United Kingdom.

Wolf

It's a little complicated, perhaps, but wolf remains popular, especially with a foursome. Choose a player to start the proceedings; this person is the wolf. Each player then takes over being the wolf on succeeding holes. The wolf always tees off first but after the next player tees off, the wolf accepts or declines having the player as a partner. The third player then tees off, and the wolf decides whether or not to have this golfer as a partner. This determines the teams for each hole and the game continues as two-man better ball. If you are part of the winning team, you get a point and the person with the most points at the end of the round wins the lucre.

Chairman

A good choice for a threesome. The first person to win a hole becomes chairman. Once you are chairman, you score a point if you win a hole. To knock you out of the chair, one of the other players must have a lower score than you on a hole. Once that happens, you must win a hole to become chairman. Often, a single point wins this one.

DEALING WITH CHEATS

There are lots of golfers who cheat. The games they play and what you can do:

Falsifying the handicap. In the United Kingdom, a handicap cheat is called a "rogue" or "bandit." In America, golfers use a different term that can't be printed in a book like this. It's remarkable, but there are plenty of serious golfers who want to win club tournaments so badly that they find ways to inflate their handicap using technicalities. If you are playing with a handicap cheat, you can say, after a big drive, "That's pretty good for a 12." This alerts the cheat that you're onto them. And when they miss a putt, you can say, "Now I know why that handicap is so high."

Wrong ball. A golfer comes out of the woods with a ball. But it's not necessarily the original one. If you think this might be happening, check the make of the ball and the mark. If the golfer hits a provisional, check the number on the ball and if the golfer finds a ball but is not sure whether it was the first or second ball, they are in trouble.

The rules ignoramus. This type of cheat actually knows the rules very well but counts on your lack of knowledge to their advantage. The best defense is to have at least a basic understanding of the key rules, such as what happens when a ball goes into a lateral water hazard. Here's what I say when someone is trying to bend the rules: "That's not how I see the rule. If I'm not sure, I give the advantage to my opponent. You do what you think is fair."

The jangler. It's not illegal, of course, to jangle change and other items in the pocket when someone else is putting but it's a clear breach of the accepted rules of etiquette. The best bet is to make all the short putts.

There's no point cheating in golf and there's a long list of excuses I make to ensure that I don't play with these golfers when they call up for a game.

TIPPING

Some general guidelines.

➤ Scottish Caddy: 40 to 60 pounds.
➤ Caddy at a big-time resort (in addition to fee, per bag): $60 to $100.
➤ Wait staff and bar staff at a resort or hotel: normal tipping applies; roughly 15 to 20 percent. In the United Kingdom, the service charge may be in the fee or cost.

LEAVE THE CART BEHIND

The object of golf is to have fun. Some might say that the object is to get the ball in the hole. However, it's more important to enjoy the outdoors, good company, and those occasional wonderful shots. Golf is even better when you walk. The rhythm of the game is much more amenable, and the exercise isn't going to kill you. If you hate carrying a bag, get a trolley. I use a contraption called a Speed Cart which is a glorified baby jogger re-engineered to carry a golf bag. It's the greatest thing since sliced bread. At some courses, you can only walk if you hire a caddy. Beautiful.

PART III

GOLF
IS FUN

GOLF JOKES

It always helps to have some golf jokes hanging around in the cranium. Here are some clean ones.

A man was standing on a tee at his club and was about to hit his drive. The tee was close to a road and offered a clear view of the road. Just before the golfer was about to tee off, a funeral procession rolled by. The golfer stopped, put his driver off to one side, and then bowed reverently until the procession passed. The golfer then hit a superb drive right down the middle of the fairway.

While walking to the ball for the next shot, one of the man's playing partners came up and said,

"That was very good of you to bow as the procession rolled along. I admire that very much. Did you know the person?"

"I certainly did. I was married to her for 30 years."

* * *

At Turnpike Meadows Golf Club, the first tee is close to a busy road. One day, a golfer is going out on a quiet round. He takes a few practice swings, then gets ready to hit the ball. Unfortunately, he hits a very nasty duck hook and the ball goes straight toward the road. The ball hits a car. The car veers off wildly and hits a pick-up truck. The pick-up truck hits a UPS van. The UPS van hits a tractor-trailer, which runs into a tanker carrying gasoline that subsequently explodes, creating a massive fireball. The tanker then plunges into the nearby harbor, where it rams into a fishing vessel.

The golfer who hit the hook, after watching the carnage and chaos, decides that he would rather retire to the bar to relieve the shock than play golf.

In the bar, the usually teetotal golfer orders a triple brandy.

"Are you sure?" asks the bartender.

"Absolutely. Hit me," says the golfer.

"Is there something wrong? You're as white as a sheet."

"I hit a bad shot on the first tee and the ball went into the road and hit a car. The car hit a pick-up and the pick-up hit a delivery van and the delivery van hit a semi and the semi hit a gas truck and the truck exploded, then went off the road into a harbor and destroyed a fishing boat."

"How did that happen?" asks the bartender.

"I hit a bad hook. What should I do?"

"Well next time, check your grip, make a more upright swing and make your tempo a little smoother and slower."

* * *

What do you call a fish that operates on the brain?

A neuro-sturgeon.

* * *

There was an explosion today at the pie factory. Did you hear about it?

3.14 people died.

* * *

An English professor was taking his first golf lesson and asked if the word putt was spelled p-u-t or p-u-t-t. The instructor said it was spelled p-u-t-t.

"That can't be," said the professor. "Put is defined as placing something exactly where you want it go. Putt means nothing of the sort."

ESSENTIAL LINES FROM CADDYSHACK

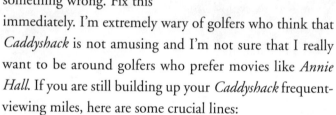

If you're a golfer and you haven't seen *Caddyshack* at least ten times, there's something wrong. Fix this immediately. I'm extremely wary of golfers who think that *Caddyshack* is not amusing and I'm not sure that I really want to be around golfers who prefer movies like *Annie Hall*. If you are still building up your *Caddyshack* frequent-viewing miles, here are some crucial lines:

Hey Wang! Quit taking pictures. It's a parking lot . . .

Hey Wang! Don't tell them you're Jewish. I think this place is restricted.

That's a peach.

Oh Dolly. I'm hot today.

There's a pool and a pond. The pond would be good for you.

I *demand* satisfaction.

How 'bout a Fresca?

That must be the tea!

Hey Moose! Rocco! Help the judge find his checkbook!

Gambling is illegal at Bushwood and I *never* slice.

TEN THINGS YOU SHOULD KNOW ABOUT CADDYSHACK

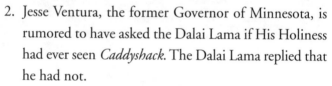

1. The Havercamps, the old couple for whom Tony caddies early in the movie, had never acted before.

2. Jesse Ventura, the former Governor of Minnesota, is rumored to have asked the Dalai Lama if His Holiness had ever seen *Caddyshack*. The Dalai Lama replied that he had not.

3. Jackie Davis played Porterhouse, the locker room attendant. In real life, Davis was an accomplished recording artist and one of the first to play the Hammond Organ.

4. Spaulding is now a residential real estate agent in the Boston area.

5. Michael O'Keefe, who played Danny Noonan, has enjoyed a successful acting career and is also an ordained Buddhist priest.

6. The producers filmed *Caddyshack* primarily in South Florida at Rolling Hills, which is now Grande Oaks.

However, several scenes were shot in southern California. Remember the entrance to Bushwood? That's in Los Angeles. It is the entrance to Bel Aire Country Club on Sunset Boulevard.

7. In the French version of *Caddyshack*, the gopher is a *marmotte*.

8. The producers added all the gopher scenes well after initial filming took place. John Dykstra and his team created the gopher; Dykstra also produced the special effects for a couple of Star Wars movies.

9. Maggie O'Hooligan, the Irish girl, only appeared in two movies: *Caddyshack* and *Animal House*. The actress: Sarah Holcomb. If you ask me, that's a career right there.

10. The author whose work you are currently enjoying has written a vital book about the movie titled: *The Book of Caddyshack. Everything You Always Wanted to Know About the Greatest Movie Ever Made.* Your life will be significantly better if you purchase at least ten copies right now!

I have never seen *Caddyshack II*, but I would strongly advise you not to bother. No golf movie has ever come close to being as good as *Caddyshack*, though French-Canadian hockey players are especially fond of *Happy Gilmore*.

SCENES IN NON-GOLF MOVIES WITH WHICH YOU SHOULD HAVE SOME FAMILIARITY

Goldfinger. The match between Auric Goldfinger and James Bond is superb. In the book, it takes place at Royal St. George's. However, the producer shot the scene at Stoke Poges just west of London.

Animal House. Two members of the Delta House, Otter and Boone, practice their driving while parade is going on. Poor technique, but great golf clothes.

Carefree. Fred Astaire was a tremendous dancer, obviously, but he was also no duffer on the golf course. In *Carefree*, there's a scene where he dances *and* plays golf at the same time. In fact, he plays the harmonica, tap dances, does a Scottish reel, hits a few perfect pitches then hits several perfect drives. Look it up on YouTube.

THE GAMES GOLF COURSE ARCHITECTS PLAY

The first known golf course architect was Mother Nature, who provided the land for the Old Course at St. Andrews. The land, known as linksland, was pretty much just rough dunes covered primarily with bentgrass and dense fescues. The land, with its sandy soil, was good for grazing sheep but not much else. The sheep, huddling against the Scottish summer weather, dug out bunkers and kept the grass clipped to fairway level. At some stage, some bored shepherds decided to get a stick and make a ball and they started to play golf. The game took off more formally in the mid 18th century, yet it wasn't until Old Tom Morris started tinkering with the Old Course that the business of golf course architecture became a viable profession.

Linksland is rare these days, and it really only exists in the United Kingdom. If you want to build a golf course, the work starts with hiring a golf course architect. Many golf courses are famous, even revered, for their design, and it's not rare for a golf course architect today to charge fees upwards of $1 million for a golf course. I'm not one of the thousands of golfers who gets extremely excited about golf course architects, but I think it's valuable to know a little bit about some of the bigger names. They all have their common traits, and knowing what an architect likes can shave some strokes off your game.

Donald Ross

Ross arrived to the United States from the north of Scotland, and soon started building courses in the Boston area and in Pinehurst. Well over 600 courses bear his name. If you're playing a Ross course it's likely that another architect has come along and tinkered with it; if you want to see courses that are close to his original work, head to Pinehurst #2 or Pine Needles. In general, Ross liked wide fairways but the best line off the tee was usually close to a fairway bunker. Many Ross greens are large but several are small and some have rounded edges, especially toward the back of the green. Aim for the middle of the green. Ross wanted his bunkers taken seriously, so don't go in one! It's often a good idea to stay underneath the hole on a Ross green. Ross liked to include at least two long par-threes in his routings.

Robert Trent Jones

The biggest name in golf course architecture after World War II, original Jones courses were long and muscular at the time and still seem like backbreakers today. Original Jones courses have single teeing grounds that look like a small runway or bowling lane at the bowling alley. Greens are often large but bunkers are even bigger, often cloverleaf in shape. Just stay out of those bunkers and you'll be fine. It also helps if you can mash the ball! Jones believed that par should be difficult for the average golfer but that bogey should be relatively attainable.

Pete Dye

Originally from Indiana, Dye started in the life insurance business, and there are plenty of golfers who wished that he had stayed in that business. At first look, a Dye course seems a little wacky with all those railroad ties and bizarrely shaped greens, water hazards, and island greens; at one of his earlier courses in North Carolina, there's even an island tee. However, if you play a Dye course from the right set of tees, it can be a lot of fun. The key is ignoring all the funny features and picking the right line off the tee. From there, many Dye greens are really three greens in one, so aim for the correct part of the green on approach shots.

Alister MacKenzie

Highly revered among golf course architects, MacKenzie designed gems like Augusta National and Cypress Point, although you won't find much of his work at the former.

MacKenzie spent parts of his early career helping military types improve their camouflage techniques. He applied his knowledge to golf course architecture. Many MacKenzie courses are among the most beautiful in the world and his bunkering is among the best—unless you are in one of them.

Tom Fazio

One of the biggest names in golf course architecture, Fazio's first effort, at Lake Nona near Orlando, Florida, is quite unlike his more recent courses. I wish that were not the case, but the modern "textbook" Fazio course is not exactly chopped liver. In many ways, you'll find the best of Ross, MacKenzie, and many of the older classical golf courses, on a Fazio course. In golf architecture parlance, Fazio courses are typically strategic; this means that the courses offer options galore. If you pull off a difficult or risky shot off the tee, your reward will be an easier second shot. If you play safe, then your next shot will be harder, and so on.

While I'm not sure that knowing a ton about a golf course architect is going to take you from a 17 handicap to a 7 in a few weeks, golf becomes significantly more interesting if you know something about golf course architects.

THE
BETTER GOLF
WRITERS

Pro beach volleyball has
its devotees, and with
good reason, but per-
haps the biggest difference between pro beach volleyball
and golf is that golf has a deeper and broader literary port-
folio. If you want to read about pro beach volleyball,
there's *Order on the Court: Pro Beach Volleyball a Rally for
Respect & Recognition* by Tom Burke, or *Karch Kiraly's
Championship Volleyball* by Karch Kiraly. If you want to
read about golf, almost 270 golf books are published each
year; the subjects include history, biographies, instruction,
golf course architecture, and travel. There's even, and I'm
not joking, a book about the tee. That's right: a gentleman
wrote almost 200 pages about the history of the little white
thing that we stick in the ground when we tee off.

Here's a brief guide to some of the better golf writers.
To my knowledge, none of them has written a history of
the tee.

Herbert Warren Wind

Wind wrote about golf primarily for *The New Yorker* magazine. Thankfully, *The New Yorker* had plenty of space available for his work as Wind certainly knew how to type, and if *The New Yorker* paid him by the word then Wind must have been a multi-billionaire. So, you need some time to take in Wind's work but in this day and age of texting and blogging, it's actually refreshing to read the work of a writer who was in no hurry. It's not that Wind's work was wordy just for the sake of pumping out words: Wind chose his subjects carefully and his articles are fascinating, providing superb insight into post-World War II golf in the United States. Wind wrote several stand-alone books and several publishers have published compilations of his work.

Bernard Darwin

Darwin was Charles Darwin's grandson and was an excellent golfer; he was captain of the Cambridge University golf team. Darwin's primary writing gig was golf correspondent for the *Times*; he also wrote for the British magazine *Country Life*. Darwin was a prolific author and every golfer should make the effort to read *Bernard Darwin on Golf*. Darwin was perhaps more of a stylist than the often straightforward Wind, but both shared a passion for detail and the great characters of the game. Darwin wrote extensively about golf courses in the United Kingdom and this work is a must for anyone who is even remotely interested in golf course architecture.

Peter Dobereiner

To Dobereiner, Seve Ballesteros was not Seve Ballesteros but The Pirate From Spain. To Dobereiner, golf in Italy was special because the main attraction of a day at an Italian golf course was the lunch between nines. To Dobereiner, the rules of golf were not confusing but a constant source of amusement. To Dobereiner, a golfing disaster was something to be celebrated just in case we started to take the game a little too seriously. Dobereiner is perhaps the funniest golf writer to have put pen to paper, though he clearly took the game and its stature seriously. But not too seriously. He loved the characters of the game and their shenanigans, and he lived at a time when golf writers (and most journalists) were expected to file a good story then indulge in plenty of "refreshment" with locals, other writers, and even the golfers they covered. Dobereiner liked his red wine, and who could blame him? Newspapers paid him to travel around the finest parts of Europe to follow the circus that was the European Tour in the 60s and 70s, and if you're covering a golf tournament in Umbria and you're not enjoying a robust Super Tuscan, then you must be a corpse. Dobereiner referred to white wine as "battery acid," but he was careful to avoid causticity when writing about professional golfers.

Today's golf writers will mercilessly bash a touring professional for missing a three-foot putt at a big moment but Dobereiner, perhaps because he was friends with so many of the players, was more consoling. He knew that golf could be hard on the soul and was more likely to commiserate than criticize. Dobereiner is at his best when writing about the characters *in* the game and the character *of* the game, especially from his wonderful point of view. The golf writers I know take themselves very seriously. Peter Dobereiner inspires a love for the game part of the game of golf, and every golfer who loves golf more for the camaraderie, the people, and the utter nonsense that sometimes goes along with the game should read every word he wrote.

Bobby Jones

Jones was one of the greatest players to play the game and won numerous major championships as an amateur before retiring before he was 30 to pursue his "true" professional career as a lawyer. Jones' reputation in golf is without parallel, and his writing was superb. Jones wrote primarily about technique and strategy. His writing is clear and his prose has a wonderful 1920s gentle and gentlemanly cadence and structure. He was not afraid of clauses and long sentences and his vocabulary was always vivid. It's a pity that his body of work is limited to just a few books. Still, all golfers should know the Bobby Jones story, despite its somewhat tragic end, and perhaps the best way to get to know the legendary golfer is through his writing.

Of the modern writers, I like Lorne Rubenstein, Tom Doak, and Michael Bamburger, but they are not in the same league as the writers above. Too many writers today are trying to be the next Dobereiner or the next Darwin instead of just being themselves. And today's golf magazines are more obsessed with celebrity and the latest driver than the pure fun and joy (and agony) of routine public and club golf.

Hopefully, you'll take some time to read the work of some of the writers I just discussed; it will get you fired up about getting out there to play some more.

GOLF SLANG (IN NO PARTICULAR ORDER)

Roseanne. Hit it fat. *I really Roseanned that one; I must have hit five inches behind the ball.*

Twiggy. Hit it thin. *A bit twiggy but it should be OK.*

Sally. An ugly shot that runs and runs. (After the runner, Sally Gunnell, who is not really that ugly.)

Fuhrer. Two shots in the bunker.

Damian. Three sixes in a row on the scorecard. *A six on the par-three, a six on the par-four, and a six on the par-five. That's a Damian, I'm afraid.*

J. Arthur. A shank. (English: rhyming slang after J. Arthur Rank, the American entrepreneur who made a fortune in England producing movies). *He won't admit it due to his general blindness to bad shots, but Jack Nicklaus just had a J. Arthur.*

Fried egg. A ball that lands in a bunker but does not bounce, and is somewhat plugged in the sand. *Oh dear, you'll want some bacon and coffee with that fried egg.*

O. J. Bad shot but got away with it. (May no longer apply.)

Diego Maradonna. A nasty five-footer.

Rock Hudson. A putt that looked straight but was not. *I hit the putt right where I wanted it but it dove off to the left at the end. A Rock Hudson if ever I've seen one.*

Salman Rushdie. A putt that's impossible to read.

Dance Floor. The green. *It wasn't a great shot, but it's dancing!*

Jungle. Really bad rough. *You're in the jungle again . . . you'll never find that.*

Army golf. Left then right, all over the golf course.

Jammy. Lucky (Scottish).

Snowman. Eight on the scorecard.

Back door. Putt that goes in the back of the hole.

All-around good putt. A putt that circles the entire rim of the hole and then goes in.

Hormel. Hit a fat shot (i.e. cover/smother it).

Dawn patrol. Golfers who regularly get up very early.

Rabbit. A very poor, timid, and weak player. *I hope you don't mind playing with me, I'm a real rabbit.*

Rake it back. Concede a putt.

Wormburner. Low shot. *It looks like a wormburner but I was just trying to keep it under the wind.*

Obama. A shot that skips over the water onto dry land.

Skinful. A lot of beer. *I was not playing so well after lunch. Perhaps it was the effect of the skinful I had with my leek soup.*

Golf slang is a tremendously entertaining part of the game, and part of the joy of traveling is learning new golf slang, or just slang in general. For example, in Scotland, you might be telling a story to a local who clearly does not believe a word you are saying. At the end of the story, the listener might say: "and then yer erse fell off."

YOU HAVE A HOLE-IN-ONE!

Drinks are on you in the clubhouse. Tell the professional in the shop and they will call up the newspaper.

YOU'VE WON THE GAME

After collecting, the first round of drinks in the clubhouse is on you.

THE STARSHIP ENTERPRISE HAS BEAMED YOU TO . . .

Pinehurst

If you're in this southern slice of paradise, here are some general thoughts.

➤ Play Pinehurst #2, but also one of the lesser-known courses like #1.
➤ Avoid #7; it's overrated and not worth the extra money.
➤ Take 30 minutes to walk up and down the main hallway in the clubhouse.
➤ Go to the Pine Crest Inn.
➤ Take a caddy.
➤ Don't panic if #2 beats you up at first; it's a tremendously difficult course.

➤ Play Pinehurst #8, as it's perhaps the best of Tom Fazio's courses in the Carolinas.

➤ Pinehurst is actually the resort itself. However, when visiting one of the approximately 35 courses in the area, most people say, "I'm going to Pinehurst."

➤ Spend some time in the bar at The Pine Crest Inn. Dinner is also very good there.

If you are in the area and you want to get off-campus, here are some courses you should play: Foxfire (excellent value), Pine Needles, Mid Pines, Forest Creek (private), and the Country Club of North Carolina (private).

For more information about Pinehurst:

Pinehurst Resort and Country Club
One Carolina Vista Drive
Village of Pinehurst
North Carolina 28374
800.ITS.GOLF/910.235.8507
Pinehurst.com

THE STARSHIP ENTERPRISE HAS BEAMED YOU TO . . .

Pebble Beach

You're in one of the most magnificent golf destinations on the planet. Here are some general thoughts.

➤ You're going to find it tough to leave. Everyone says it's hard to get back in the car or get back on an airplane.

➤ The weather can be frisky. Be prepared.

➤ The courses around here have poa annua greens that can get bumpy and unpredictable at the end of the day.

➤ Take a caddy.

➤ The drive from San Francisco is about three hours, a little less if there's no traffic.

➤ There are four courses at Pebble Beach and they are all among the finest in the country: Pebble Beach Golf Links, The Links at Spanish Bay, Spyglass Hill Golf

Course, and Del Monte Golf Course. There's also a short 'Executive' nine-hole course called Peter Hay.

➤ There are seven places to eat.

➤ The two main places to stay are the Lodge and the Inn at Spanish Bay.

➤ Off-campus, try Casanova in Carmel; it has close to 30,000 bottles of wine.

➤ Book well ahead.

➤ Be prepared for a slow round, especially on The Links at Pebble Beach.

➤ Bring your non-golf playing spouse; they won't be disappointed.

If you want more information, here you go:

Pebble Beach Resorts
1700 17-Mile Drive
Pebble Beach CA 93953
(800) 654-9300
pebblebeach.com

THE STARSHIP ENTERPRISE HAS BEAMED YOU TO...

Bandon Dunes

Bandon Dunes is a mere baby, an infant really, in the golf world yet it looks like it's been there forever. Some key points:

➤ The land is as close to the real thing as you'll find outside of Scotland: dunes and linksland on the coast of Oregon.

➤ The nearest airport, which has only minimal service, is about 30 minutes away. You can fly into Eugene or Portland but you really need to take a full travel day, either way you go.

➤ The golf course architects are all devotees of classical architecture.

➤ Bandon is walking only; caddies are available.

➤ From the first pages of the Yardage Book at the Bandon Dunes course that Bill Coore and Ben Crenshaw designed:

"As its name implies, Bandon Trails will take you on a walk if you will, through windswept dunes, meadows of vegetation framed by indigenous shrubbery, and through woodlands of towering fir and spruce trees. Sometimes the journey and the golf will be wild and tumultuous, sometimes serene."

➤ Get ready for 36 holes a day. There's not much else at Bandon Dunes, and you'll want to work up an appetite so that you can enjoy the excellent dining plus the microbrews in McKee's Pub.

➤ You'll get a chance to hit some links-type shots at Bandon Dunes. Go ahead and hit the shots! Have a go!

If you need more information . . .

Bandon Dunes Golf Resort
57744 Round Lake Drive
Bandon, Oregon 97411
541-347-4380
888-345-6008
bandondunesgolf.com

THE STARSHIP ENTERPRISE HAS BEAMED YOU TO ...

Scotland (for a couple of weeks)

Scotland is the home of golf, and every golfer should make the effort to get there at least once. Here are some general thoughts should you get the chance to visit and play some golf there:

➤ The best time of year to visit Scotland is summer, not because the weather is any better than it might be in February but because you get long days when the sun will come up at around 4 A.M. and not set until around midnight. Three rounds in a day? No problem at all.

➤ Famous courses are fun to visit, but be warned that they are not always the best courses and they are the most expensive by far.

➤ East coast courses tend to be "bouncier" than west coast courses because the east coast tends to get less rain.

➤ Take caddies wherever you go, but don't expect them to be "service oriented" and trained in tact. That's part of the fun.

➤ At several courses, the rough can be very rough and you'll lose your ball if you leave the fairway. So use common sense and take a wood or hybrid off the tee so that you can keep moving.

➤ Don't be surprised to find some greens that aren't up to the standard at your course at home. Clubs usually leave their greenskeeping up to Mother Nature.

➤ You're going to find plenty of blind shots. Get used to it and learn to enjoy the suspense. Or something like that!

➤ You'll find the quirkiest and most interesting Scottish golf courses near or totally off the beaten path. Find these courses if you really want to enjoy the golf.

➤ Have a night at a local pub that's not part of the golf club or golf course.

➤ Many golf groups (too many) have unrealistic itineraries. They stay night-to-night, cram 36 holes in, and travel like a nascent rock band. The result is total fatigue. If you can, break up your trip so that you spend a few days in one location, then move to the next stop.

➤ Have haggis and black pudding at least once. Sausage-lovers will love British sausages.

➤ Scots drink very mediocre lager, a lot of Guinness, plus a version of English bitter they call "Heavy."

➤ To get a guaranteed spot on the Old Course, you need to book well ahead (at least 18 months), book through a travel specialist with access to tee times, or go through the "St. Andrews Experience."

➤ You save thousands of dollars by organizing the tour yourself, but it will take hours and hours of time. It's not easy, and that's why so many golfers take the sensible step of getting a golf tour specialist to put together the trip.

➤ An increasingly large number of people are joining a golf club in Scotland and eschewing the "grand tour" for a week of relative peace and relaxation in one spot.

➤ Often, your golf professional will organize a trip for members. This can be an excellent way of making a golf trip relatively easy.

There are no rights and wrongs when it comes to a golf tour of Scotland, and it's a place that every golfer should visit.

For more information about St. Andrews . . .

St. Andrews Links Trust
Pilmour House
St. Andrews
Fife KY16 9SF
Scotland
+44 (0) 1334 466666
standrews.org.uk

For further information about Scotland as a whole, visit www.visitscotland.com.

THE STARSHIP ENTERPRISE HAS BEAMED YOU TO . . .

Casa de Campo in the Dominican Republic

Golf in the Caribbean has typically been somewhat spotty when it comes to quality and that's changing with advances in agronomy, but one place that's always been one of the world's top golf destinations is Casa de Campo. Here's what you need to know.

➤ Fly straight to Casa de Campo or to Las Americas International Airport in Santo Domingo, about 90 minutes from the resort.

➤ Casa de Campo (house in the country) has three golf courses.

➤ Casa de Campo is a family-friendly resort.

➤ Pete Dye built the main courses at Casa de Campo and called it Teeth of the Dog. It's one of Pete Dye's earliest golf courses, built in 1971.

➤ Construction took about 18 months, and laborers used oxen to transport materials.

➤ Employ one of the many caddies.

➤ After the round head for a pub called "The Pub."

If you like the Caribbean but have always wanted to get some good golf in, you can't go wrong with Casa de Campo.

For more information:

Casa de Campo
P.O. Box 140
La Romana
Dominican Republic
(800) 877-3643
casadecampo.com.do

THE STARSHIP ENTERPRISE HAS BEAMED YOU TO . . .

South Florida

Whether it's the azure skies in the winter months, the soothing breezes in the summer, or the kaleidoscopic clash of cultures, there's something very special about South Florida. The golf is undoubtedly at its best in the late fall until early spring and there's lot of it, usually next to some type of sumptuous resort.

Here are some places that should be on your "must visit" list if you're heading to South Florida:

The Ritz-Carlton Sarasota. (941) 309-2000. ritzcarlton.com.

A newer property, but totally resplendent. Really good new Tom Fazio golf course where the earth movers went slightly bananas.

Doral Resort and Spa. (800) 713-6725.
doralresort.com.

Home of the Blue Monster, and several wonderful old-school South Florida golf courses. The resort itself is pleasant enough and it's the home of The Jim McLean Golf School. The new(ish) Great White Course is fun.

Boca Raton Resort and Club. 888-491-BOCA.
Bocaresort.com.

A stunning and palatial main property along with numerous amenities and tremendous golf; there's even a half-mile of private beach. It's the spot where the legendary Tommy Armour used to teach while perched under an umbrella enjoying a cocktail or two.

THE STARSHIP ENTERPRISE HAS BEAMED YOU TO . . .

London

. . . and beamed your golf clubs as well. Thanks Mr. Scott!

The London area boasts some of the finest inland golf on the planet. So, if your travels take you there, make sure that you bring your golf clubs. Most of the best of the golf is to the west, southwest, and south of London where the land is gently rolling and the soil is mostly sandy. It's called heathland and it is comprised of woods, heather, ferns, and generally magnificent scenery.

Note that most of the clubs are private but most are accessible. The key is a well-written letter to the secretary of the club; the secretary is not an administrative person *per se* but the person who is ultimately in charge of running the club . . . and deciding who gets on and who does not! Harry

Shapland Colt designed many of the golf courses around London, and he was an immensely talented architect who was given some phenomenal pieces of property.

Here are a few of the courses you should strive to visit:

Swinley Forest. One of the most private courses in the United Kingdom, some call it the Augusta National of England. I would put it this way: Augusta National is the Swinley Forest of the United States. Or at least it comes close. But remember that the first and last holes at Swinley are totally mediocre.

New Zealand Golf Club. Quirky and sporty with a quirky and sporty membership.

Royal Ashdown Forest. A "what you see is what you get" course built in 1891 and mostly unchanged. It's a hillier course with lovely, peaceful views from the higher holes. There are no bunkers on the course because it's on land that the Queen owns. The small bar has a few benches around the exterior and is very welcoming.

Sunningdale. Is there a club in the world with a better brace of courses? I'd like to find it. The Old and the New Course at Sunningdale are superb. See if you can organize a day of it with golf in the morning, a big lunch, and then golf in the afternoon. The sausages at the halfway hut are the finest in the universe.

Wentworth. Have you watched the World Match Play Championships? It takes place at Wentworth. It's the most corporate and polished of all the clubs in the area and they have three courses now.

West Sussex. Charming and welcoming, it rests on a beautiful piece of property. Like many British clubs, it's known by the name of the adjacent town, in this case, Pulborough. Challenging, elegant, with a fine finishing hole.

Planning a trip to London is always a worthwhile venture, but it's particularly exciting if you can bring your golf clubs. Getting onto some of the courses in the area requires some effort but if you get a fine day, it's worth it. September and October are the best times to visit although you can't go wrong in the summer.

A SENSE OF REALITY FROM BEN HOGAN

The great Ben Hogan
said that he only really
hit two or three shots a round he thought were close to perfect. So please be realistic about your ball-striking expectations, and be delighted to be out there in the beauty of the
golf course.

THE ODDS OF MAKING A HOLE-IN-ONE

The odds of making a hole-in-one are slim. To be precise, they are approximately 1.2 million to one. Or about the same as Metallica playing a Nancy Sinatra song on their next tour. Quite often, at a charity golf tournament, the organizers will organize a hole where you might win a car if you get a hole-in-one. The tournament organizers or the car dealer that supplied the car usually purchases insurance in case someone actually makes a hole-in-one, but I often wonder why.